Annette Roeder & Pamela Baron

The Power of Architecture

25 Modern Buildings from around the World

PRESTEL

Munich · London · New York

**A world of
modern buildings!**
page 4

1 Unité d'Habitation

Marseille, France
and Berlin, Germany
page 6

**2 TWA Flight Center,
New York**

New York, USA
page 8

**3 Jean-Marie Tjibaou
Cultural Center**

Nouméa, New Caledonia
in the South Pacific
page 10

4 SESC Pompéia

São Paulo, Brazil
page 12

5 Munich Olympic Stadium

Munich, Germany
page 14

**6 New Museum of
Contemporary Art**

New York, USA
page 16

7 Steilneset Memorial

Vardø, Norway
page 18

8 Gosplan Garage

Moscow, Russia
page 20

9 Fallingwater

Mill Run, USA
page 22

10 CopenHill / Amager Bakke

Copenhagen, Denmark
page 24

**11 Battersea Power
Station**

London, United Kingdom
page 26

12 Dirty House

London, United Kingdom
page 28

13 Franklin Court

Philadelphia, USA
page 30

14 Sharp Center for Design
Toronto, Canada
page 32

15 Einstein Tower
Potsdam, Germany
page 34

16 Elbe Philharmonic Hall
Hamburg, Germany
page 36

17 Dandaji Regional Market
Dandaji, Niger
page 38

**18 Lycée Schorge
Secondary School**
Koudougou, Burkina Faso
page 40

19 Port House Antwerp
Antwerp, Belgium
page 42

20 Amdavad ni Gufa
Ahmedabad, India
page 44

21 Fagus Factory
Alfeld, Germany
page 46

22 Sydney Opera House
Sydney, Australia
page 48

23 Shelter of Cardboard
Location: Wherever
it is needed
page 50

24 Tree House
Singapore
page 52

**25 Micro Yuan'er
Children's Library**
Beijing, China
page 54

The **buildings**
in this book
page 56

The **architects**
in this book
page 56

A world of modern buildings!

Take a quick look out your window. Maybe you see a shaggy dog, a gray cat, or a few people walking past? Maybe you see a city skyline, a meadowland, a tree, or some bicycles? Whatever the case, there's likely to be something very close nearby that people have built... just like the house you're living in right now! All of these buildings are called architecture! This word comes from an ancient Greek term meaning "supreme builder."

People have been building their environment for almost as long as they could walk on two legs. In other words, for more than 370,000 years. We build for many different reasons: to have a roof over our heads, to cross a river, to bury the dead, or to look into the distance. Some buidings are used for offices, for celebrations, for concerts and plays, for art exhibits, or for playing sports without getting soaking wet. Other buildings are designed for learning, reading, and thinking; for sending rockets into space; for housing elephants; or for healing the sick. I'm sure you can think of many, many more things that can be done in a building. You can even make your own building just for fun... maybe with Lego bricks or wooden building blocks?

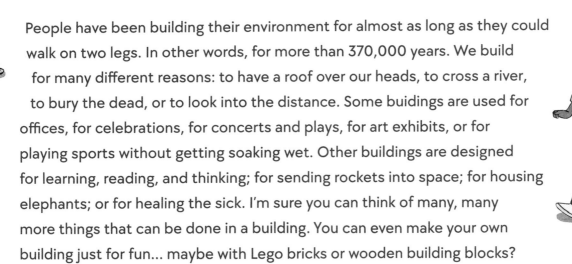

Building materials are just as diverse as the reasons for using them in the first place. You might build with materials that have been quarried from the ground, such as stone, or those that have grown out of the soil, such as wood, bamboo, or reeds. You might also use materials one wouldn't expect, like paper or felt. Some building materials have to be manufactured in ways that can harm the environment, including aluminum, steel, plastics, bricks, cement, and concrete. But there are also materials that can be taken from other places and simply reused. These recycled materials are much less damaging to the planet!

With so many types of materials and building purposes out there, it's no wonder that buildings have a variety of "looks." Many structures reveal the purpose they serve from the outside. Some look like stand-alone works of art, while others appear humble, yet serve a great purpose. Architecture comes in many colors, both on the outside and the inside. That's because there is rarely any right or wrong when it comes to building design. Nonetheless, you may find some houses more beautiful than others. You may also feel more comfortable in them. Is that because of the door handles, the light in the bathroom, the shape of the stairs or the height of the room? Only you can find that out. Take your time and think about it.

In this book, we'll explore 25 modern buildings that I find especially successful. I haven't arranged them in any particular order, but at the end of the book, you will find them again on a timeline, arranged according to their dates of construction. This section will also provide basic facts for all the buildings. One thing is for certain: it wasn't easy for me to choose only 25 examples!

My favorite architecture is scattered all over the world and serves a wide variety of purposes – from a waste incinerator to a witch memorial. Construction costs range from almost nothing to more than $860 million. The newest building was completed just as I finished this selection. And the oldest ones among them have been around for more than a century. During the 1900's, there was the so-called classical modernist period, during which a few architects questioned everything conventional and began to think about building in a completely new way. These well-known architects were almost exclusively white men until about the middle of the century. Nowadays, designing great architecture really has nothing to do with gender or skin color. You will see that when you read through the resumes of our "building people" at the very end. Artist Pamela Baron has drawn all of the buildings for you and painted them in delicate water colors. Seeing them this way may help you recognize what is special about each one. I hope you like all 25 as much as I do!

Annette Roeder

Unité d'Habitation

An apartment building like a beehive

Opinions about this famous apartment block have changed over the years. Nowadays, it has become a rather fashionable address and is loved by art connoisseurs. A replica of one of its two-story apartments even managed to get into a museum! In earlier times, however, people moved into the one of Unités because they could not afford better apartments. Residents of Marseille even called it *le truc de fada*—"the trick of the crazies!" Architect Le Corbusier presented his first designs for this "Living Machine" as early as 1925. To create as much inexpensive living space as possible, he devised a seven-story miniature "city" on thick stilts that could be erected anywhere. Three hundred and thirty seven nest-like *maisonettes*, equipped with lots of built-in furniture and open plan kitchens, were to be arranged along theatrically illuminated corridors. Le Corbusier also planned for a floor of shops in the center of the building, including a laundry and hair salon. In addition, he put a kindergarten, theater, and gym on the roof. Unité d'Habitation was constructed four times in France and once in Germany. Two of the buildings survive to this day, and anyone who manages to grab hold of an apartment in the affection- ately named "Le Corbü" is sure to be delighted.

EXPERT KNOWLEDGE

The word maisonette *comes from a French term meaning "little house." For Le Corbusier, however, a maisonette is a two-floor apartment connected by a stairwell.*

TWA Flight Center, New York

An airport terminal like a big bird

According to legend, Finnish architect Eero Saarinen came upon the idea for this building at breakfast as he was looking at a grapefruit. He placed the spooned-out peel on the table and squeezed it together. From this image, Eero designed one of the most elegant airport terminals in the world. The lattice roofs above the TWA Flight Center at New York's JFK International Airport are like the wings of a white bird. When Trans World Airlines (TWA) commissioned Saarinen to design this work in the mid-1950s, JFK was known as Idlewild airport. All the major airline companies built their own terminals at Idlewild during this time, but TWA's terminal became the most famous.

The building is a true eye-catcher from the outside, and on the inside, travelers walk along pathways that are also constructed in flowing shapes. Conveyor belts, electric sliding doors, and electronic luggage scales enable walking distances to be shortened.

The architect and his staff had to observe the goings-on at an airport before they made their designs. Everything had to be as modern as possible for the opening in 1962.

Airplane technology, however, would soon make Eero's beautiful building obsolete. Jumbo jets were being developed, and they carried many more passengers than earlier airplanes could. This development meant that the TWA check-in hall became too small to accommodate all the extra passengers. Eventually, the terminal was replaced by larger ones. Maybe, if people paid more attention to nature and only traveled by air when necessary, the TWA Flight Center at JFK airport would be the perfect size again!

TIP

You can still visit Eero Saarinen's terminal. It is now a hotel that has been faithfully renovated with furniture designed by the architect.

Jean-Marie Tjibaou Cultural Center

A new cultural center for the island

By studying the culture of the South Pacific Kanak people, architect Renzo Piano realized that doing is just as important as getting things done. He demonstrated this point of view by designing a complex that looks almost unfinished. The Tjibaou Cultural Center near Nouméa in New Caledonia looks like a Kanak village that is still being built.

The indigenous people of this South Pacific island construct their well-ventilated huts from local Iroko wood. Renzo Piano used some of the same Kanak materials and shell-like building shapes in Tjibaou, along with modern materials and technologies.

In ten gigantic huts at the center, you can now learn everything about Kanak culture by following a trail of native plants, visiting exhibitions, or watching performances. Many old trees were transplanted here, together with new ones that were planted to connect the architecture with nature.

SESC Pompéia

Brazilian architect Lina Bo Bardi is rumored to have said a strange thing about her two major building projects: "I want the SESC to be even uglier than the MASP!"

For those who don't know the MASP is a museum of modern art right in the middle of São Paulo, Brazil. And the SESC is a large leisure and cultural center with five sports fields, a swimming pool, and a library. In the 1970s, Lina Bo Bardi was commissioned to design the SESC on the site of an old steel barrel and refrigerator factory. But what she decided to do was quite unusual for that time. Bo Bardi kept the old factory halls as part of the new design, adding sports facilities and ancillary rooms in two concrete towers right next to them. Small openings (or apertures) in the towers serve as windows that look as if huge concrete moths ate into the walls. Both towers are connected on all floors by airy bridges. The SESC is now swarming with people who enjoy their leisure time in the same place where people once toiled in harsh conditions.

Lina Bo Bardi wanted to remind people of their past, even if it meant the buildings might look "ugly." This sensitive architect regarded the style of her architecture as less important than the people who used her buildings.

PAUSE FOR THOUGHT

For centuries, women were not seen as suitable architects. Why would people ever believe such a notion?

Munich Olympic Stadium

A mountain landscape made from tent roofs

Major construction projects often involve international competitions, for which architects are asked to submit their designs. Such a competition took place for the 1972 Olympic Games in Munich, Germany. New sports facilities were to be planned…but preferably not too grandiose! The office of German architect Günter Behnisch took part in the competition, which became as exciting as a crime thriller.

Late in the design process, a member of Behnisch's staff had the idea of covering the halls and stadium with a single, spacious tented roof. He had been inspired by a newspaper photo of Frei Otto's German Pavilion from the 1967 World's Fair in Montreal. Behnisch's design model was quickly recreated using some ladies' nylons and a few kebab skewers.

The hastily revamped model flopped when it was first submitted to the competition judges. However, one of the judges supported Behnisch's idea, and he convinced the city mayor to have the plan re-submitted. Ultimately, it won first prize. Frei Otto, the brilliant German engineer whose World's Fair pavilion had been inspired by soap bubbles, among other things, helped develop the Olympic stadium's complex roof, which is nearly 246,000 square feet in area. The building remains a major landmark in Munich today.

TIP

You can hike over the roof of the Munich Olympic Stadium using climbing gear and then rappel back down with a zip line!

New Museum of Contemporary Art

A museum made from building blocks

How are you supposed to accommodate a whole museum in a vacant lot of only 65 square feet? The answer is simple: pile it high! This is what Japanese architect Kazuyo Sejima and her colleague, Ryue Nishizawa, did in New York.

Six boxes made of steel girders, all covered by an aluminum lattice and illuminated during the day with strips of skylight, seem to hover above the glass ground floor.

Everything on the inside is unembellished, light gray and white.

"You can't do less," Sejima said, "Otherwise, our architecture would be invisible." Art should, after all, be the focus of attention here. Only in the bathrooms do we find architectural decoration...flower wisps can be seen on the wall tiles!

EXPERT KNOWLEDGE

When everything is reduced to a bare minimum in art and architecture, this style is known as minimalism!

Many people in Norway still dry fish on wooden frames. Such frames inspired Swiss architect Peter Zumthor to create a hanging room of remembrance. Something very terrible happened on the Norwegian island of Vardø in the 17th century. Ninety-one women and men were convicted and burned for allegedly practicing witchcraft.

Zumthor's 330-foot-long structure is made of local pine wood and covered in a white canvass, making it appear light and bright from the outside. However, when you go inside over the footbridge, it becomes very cramped and dark. For each victim there is a little window and a light bulb. Steilneset Memorial reminds people of life's contrasts: light and dark, black and white, good and evil. A cube made of steel and black glass is also part of the museum. Inside, under seven mirrors, there is a seat with eight flames shooting out of it. French-American artist Louise Bourgeois created this piece as a sculpture. Sometimes, art and architecture can explain more than words could. If you set sail for Vardø by boat, the memorial will likely be the first thing you notice when you arrive.

Steilneset Memorial

A memorial for persecuted witches

PAUSE FOR THOUGHT

Louise Bourgeois explained this memorial in one simple sentence: "Zumthor and I used earth, water, fire, and light to create views of silence." They both succeeded!

Gosplan Garage

Why be a square when you can go round?

Isn't that an incredible window? Konstantin Melnikov, the famous Russian architect, didn't just create this large, round opening to give natural light to his Gosplan Garage. It's more of a hefty sculpture that looks like an oversized car headlight. And if you look at it a bit longer, you might think the window frame is rotating. To the side of the flat garage is a four-story building for workshops and administrative offices that gives the impression of a radiator grille. Converting movement into buildings is an art form we call futurism, and futurist art was pretty bold and modern in the 1930s. Unfortunately, this was to be the last major building Melnikov completed. After that, he was no longer allowed to build anything. The government of his country, which was then called the Soviet Union, did not like modern designs. They preferred buildings that looked like classical temples. Such a pity! Who knows what Melnikov would have dreamed up next!

EXPERT KNOWLEDGE

Melnikov belonged to a group known as the Russian "avant-garde." In art, these are people who turn the old on its head, think differently from others and, as such, pave the way for new styles.

Fallingwater

The house on the waterfall

Just imagine that you own a charming piece of land in the woods. There are wondrous old trees there, and the best thing of all is the waterfall that splashes down over the rocks. You can even bathe in it during summertime! What would be nicer than to build a weekend house and look through its window at the foaming water? That's what Edgar Kaufmann from Pittsburgh was thinking when he engaged the architect, Frank Lloyd Wright. Wright was known for his organic architecture, where buildings do not distance themselves from nature but instead connect with it. Mr. Kaufmann, however, was stunned when his architect presented him with his first drafts and said: "I want you to live with the waterfall and not just look at it. It should become a part of your life." Frank Lloyd Wright did not place the house next to the waterfall, but right on it. Huge terraces on several levels hover above the river, offering perfect views of the water. Inside the house, though, you can only hear the river's soft, rustling sound. Mr. Kaufmann was quickly convinced. In the middle of his large living room perched on this sunny rock, he would dream in front of the open fireplace. He could see the treetops framed like a painting through the broad ribbon windows. And when he wanted to bathe, he simply opened the big sliding door and lowered himself straight into the stream via the hanging staircase.

TIP

There are many exciting films about Fallingwater on the internet. You can check out the individual steps of the house's construction in a computer simulation on: etereaestudios.com/works/fallingwater/

CopenHill / Amager Bakke

A garbage incinerator becomes a mountain

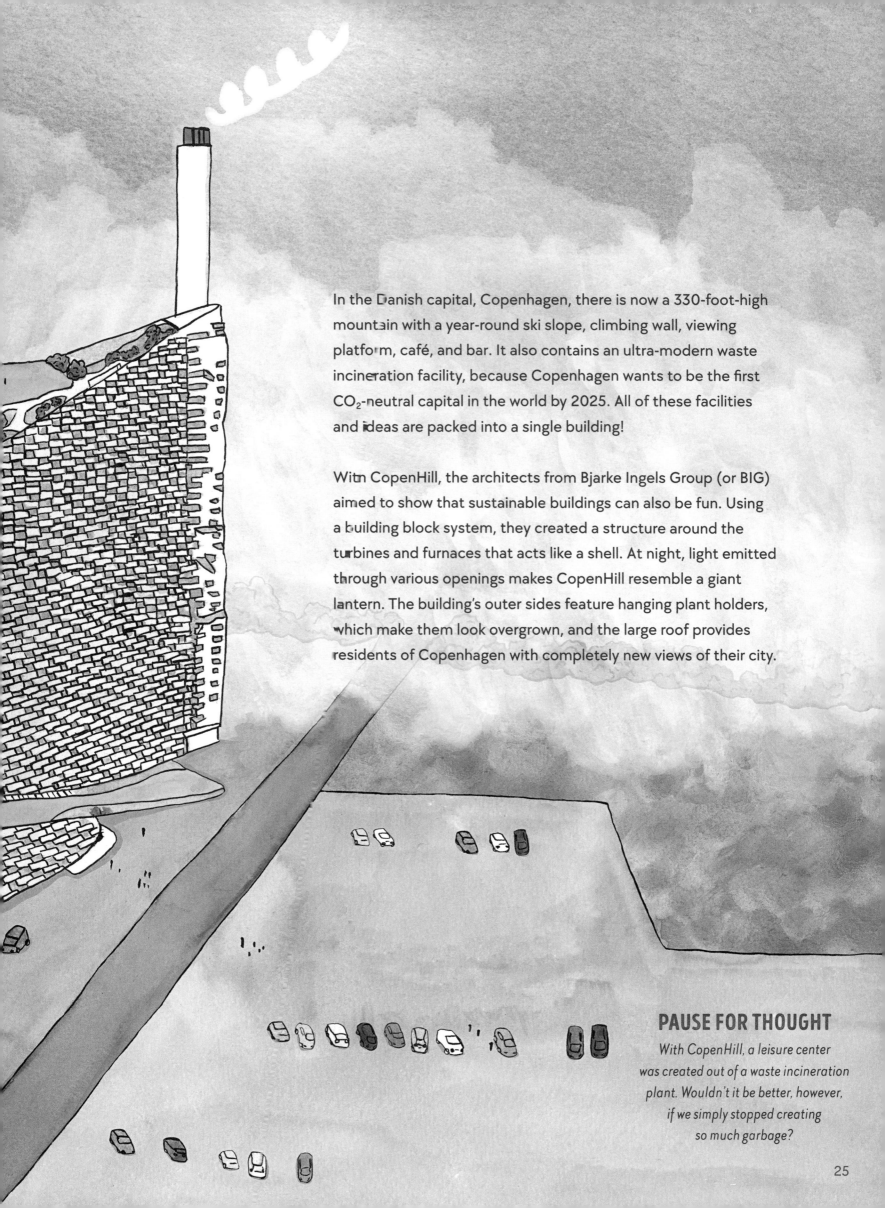

In the Danish capital, Copenhagen, there is now a 330-foot-high mountain with a year-round ski slope, climbing wall, viewing platform, café, and bar. It also contains an ultra-modern waste incineration facility, because Copenhagen wants to be the first CO_2-neutral capital in the world by 2025. All of these facilities and ideas are packed into a single building!

With CopenHill, the architects from Bjarke Ingels Group (or BIG) aimed to show that sustainable buildings can also be fun. Using a building block system, they created a structure around the turbines and furnaces that acts like a shell. At night, light emitted through various openings makes CopenHill resemble a giant lantern. The building's outer sides feature hanging plant holders, which make them look overgrown, and the large roof provides residents of Copenhagen with completely new views of their city.

PAUSE FOR THOUGHT

With CopenHill, a leisure center was created out of a waste incineration plant. Wouldn't it be better, however, if we simply stopped creating so much garbage?

Battersea Power Station

A power station gets a new purpose

Looking at it from a distance, you might easily think that Battersea Power Station is a huge church or mosque. But this gigantic brick building in the middle of London, with its four huge chimneys, is nothing more than a heat and power plant—at least that's what it was when it first opened in 1933.

After 55 years of burning coal, the plant's boilers and furnaces were removed in 1988. By that time, it had become possible to generate energy in a much less environmentally harmful way. Battersea Power Station was almost demolished.

However, many people objected because the building's memorable shape had long since become an integral part of the London cityscape, and had inspired many artists to create important films and images. Nowadays, offices, apartments, shops and restaurants are housed in this former carbon cathedral. And Battersea Power Station is not the only London building of its type to get a major makeover. Bankside Power Station was converted into the famous Tate Modern art museum.

Both buildings were originally designed by British architect Giles Gilbert Scott, the man who also designed Britain's legendary red telephone booths!

TIP

You can check out more information on Battersea Power Station at:
batterseapowerstation.co.uk

Dirty House

A house of bitter chocolate

"Architecture is white," laments Sir David Adjaye, who is the first Black architect to be knighted in the United Kingdom. He received this honor for his "dark houses," which have nicknames such as "dirty", "sunken", and "lost."

At first glance, Dirty House looks unfinished. It also invites us to ask some important questions. Where is the front door? It's hidden, like the rest of the brick wall, under bitter chocolate–brown paintwork. Is that a giant hedgehog in the window on the first floor? No... It's merely a reflection of graffiti on the opposite façade! Why does the roof hover over the balcony like a layer of icing? That's because light steel rods elevate it between the long glass walls. The light color of the roof also contrasts dramatically with the dark walls, making it appear to glow from the inside.

And who lives in such a bewildering house? That would be artists Sue Webster and Tim Noble, who moved their family and studio here. They had asked their friend David to convert an old warehouse for them. And now they have a house in the color of bitter chocolate. It looks more tasty than "dirty", don't you think? None of Sir David's buildings, by the way, are truly black!

TIP

Try mixing your darkest red, green and blue paints together. Then look at this almost black paint in different shades of light!

"Less is more" is probably the best-known statement in modern architecture. It comes from German architect Ludwig Mies van der Rohe, and it's almost one hundred years old. Mies wanted architecture to have clear geometric forms instead of the gingerbread trimmings that were fashionable during his youth. He also helped shaped an opinion that would hold firm over many years: modern buildings should demonstrate nothing more than their function. Architecture should be fun and surprise people!

But then, in the 1960s, the architect couple of Denise Scott Brown and Robert Venturi turned everything on its head by saying: "Less is a bore!" They wanted architecture that made people think about many things, including history and popular culture. Venturi and Scott Brown had a special idea for the memorial site for Benjamin Franklin, who was one of the founding fathers of the USA. They 'reconstructed' Franklin's home and printworks, which had been demolished in 1812, as steel frame outlines.
Below these 'ghost houses' was
built an underground museum.
Visitors now move—in the
present and the past.

Franklin Court

A ghostly memorial

Sharp Center for Design

A university building with colorful legs

"Courageous, bold and a little insane" was how judges from the Royal Institute of British Architects described Will Alsop's extension for the Ontario College of Design and Art in Toronto. These judges then gave him the most important British prize for architecture, the RIBA Award.

Alsop's structure really does look a bit crazy. A black-and-white pixilated box, placed on thin, 85-foot-high columns, hovers above the old university building and looks something like a bizarre animal. This type of structure opens up a lot of free space on the ground for the neighborhood, and it creates a huge gateway into a park at the same time. Alsop's building, called the Sharp Center for Design, houses studios, lecture halls, exhibition rooms, and offices. It also has extra-deep window recesses in which students can sit, lie down, and sleep. Alsop wanted to give the students places outside their work stations where they could meet and share creative ideas.

When designing the Sharp Center, Alsop ran workshops in which students and other users of the center were asked to submit ideas about what they wanted in the building. He then used these ideas to develop the design we see today. People either love or hate his building, and that's the way the architect likes it. The main thing is that they care enough to have an opinion!

TIP

Get some paper and crayons and just start drawing. Then, see if the picture you made gives you any ideas for designing a crazy house!

Einstein Tower

An observatory like a submarine

Fortunately, when this remarkable building was constructed, it stood in a somewhat remote location. That's the main reason why the Prussian Building Office consented to its "unusual and rather haphazard" shape and approved the project. Otherwise, Erich Mendelsohn's Einstein Tower would never have existed, and the world would have been deprived of a masterpiece of modern architecture! Scientists also value the tower within a tower, whose dome when opened allows the sunlight to be directed via a mirror into an underground space and then scientifically analyzed. To make the inner tower more stable, it was built to stand on its own foundations. The original idea for the tower came from scientists, including German astronomer Erwin Freundlich.

They wanted to create a solar observatory to verify theories by German physicist Albert Einstein. These theories included ideas about energy produced by the sun. Freundlich brought German architect Erich Mendelsohn on board as the architect. For this project, Mendelsohn wanted to make use of a material that was new at the time: reinforced concrete. However, problems during construction meant that traditional bricks had to be used to help stabilize the structure. Einstein Tower, which almost looks like the top of a submarine, became so famous that there is even a copy of it in China!

Elbe Philharmonic Hall

A concert hall like a flint stone

A shipwreck with torn sails, an iceberg, cresting waves, a cracked flint stone: we associate many things with the sea! Elbe Philharmonic Hall in Hamburg, Germany, stimulates the imagination like few other buildings, which was the goal of the people who built it.

Its architects, Jacques Herzog and Pierre de Meuron, designed a glass structure that towers 365 feet above the river Elbe on the walls of an old warehouse from 1963. The complex contains concert halls, a hotel, restaurants and fashionable apartments. Its upper part, which looks a bit like a cracked piece of sea flint, consists of specially curved glass panes that can only be cleaned by trained façade climbers. Such cleanings are very expensive. Each one costs about 50,000 Euros (or $54,000)! Known locally as the "Elfi," the building was many times more expensive to construct than planned, because so many custom-made materials were required. But the investment was well worth it!

TIP

*Concert tickets are not easy to come by at the Elfi.
However, you can always book a free ticket to the
observation deck and then ride on the 270-foot-long
curved escalators to the plaza!*

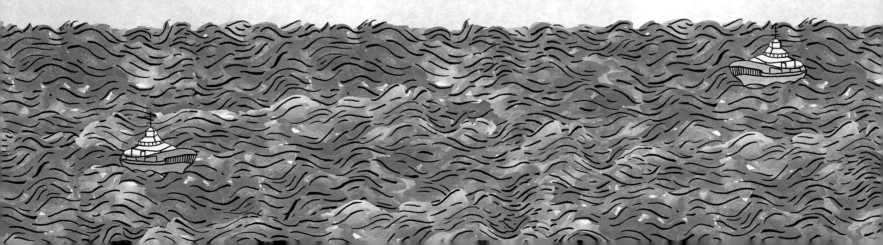

Dandaji Regional Market

A street market of scrap metal lily pads

There are many weekly markets in
Niger, with traders moving from village to village.
But in the little village of Dandaji, something has been built
that encourages people to stay. It's a market square with
sunroofs covering more than fifty-two open stalls.

Designed by Nigerien architect Mariam
Kamara, the market is made to be durable. Its walls feature compressed earth blocks (CEBs), or bricks made of compressed soil. These bricks
do not disintegrate when it rains, like traditional Nigerien mud bricks do; also, making
them does not produce environmentally damaging CO_2, as is the case with many modern
materials. For the structure, Kamara designed roofs of recycled metal, which
do not weather as quickly as traditional canopies made of plant reeds. The roofs
are mounted at different heights so that accumulated hot air can be
drawn upwards and cooler air can flow in from below.

In addition, the whole market is grouped
around an amphitheater, in the middle of which stands the
ancestral tree of the village. All in all, Dandaji Regional Market is
a great place for customers and traders to come together.
It also helps protect our environment.

Lycée Schorge Secondary School

School can be so beautiful!

Can traditional building methods also be forward-looking? Of course they can! A great example of this can be seen at the Lycée Schorge, a secondary school in Burkina Faso designed by Burkinabé architect Diébédo Francis Kéré. Nine buildings consisting of classrooms, administration offices, and even a small dental clinic loosely surround a large, open inner courtyard. The walls are made of laterite rock, which is quarried on site and air hardened. The classrooms are well ventilated with a combination of a protruding, corrugated tin roof and large wind-blocking towers. An external second façade made of wooden poles, lined up like a privacy mat, brings additional shade. The furniture is made of local wood, as well as anything left over from the roof. Why should things be thrown away when they can be used again?

In the second largest port in Europe, an old fire station was due to be remodeled into a government building for 500 employees. British-Iraqi architect Zaha Hadid won the bid for this project. She had already become world famous for her futuristic designs, which, coincidentally, included a fire station.

In Zaha Hadid's architecture, gravity often does not seem to exist, with walls and roofs just whizzing through the air like arrows! You can see this aspect of her style in the Port House of Antwerp, Belgium. A sparkling "diamond" made of glass triangles on three concrete supports hovers above the old fire station house. It can be reached using elegant glass elevators. In this way, old and new are brought together. The walls of the old fire station remain and seem, to a certain extent, to be completed by the overhanging superstructure. Port House's original plan also provided for a tower, so that the building could be seen from above.
But even without the tower,
this "flying" architecture
makes a remarkable
impression!

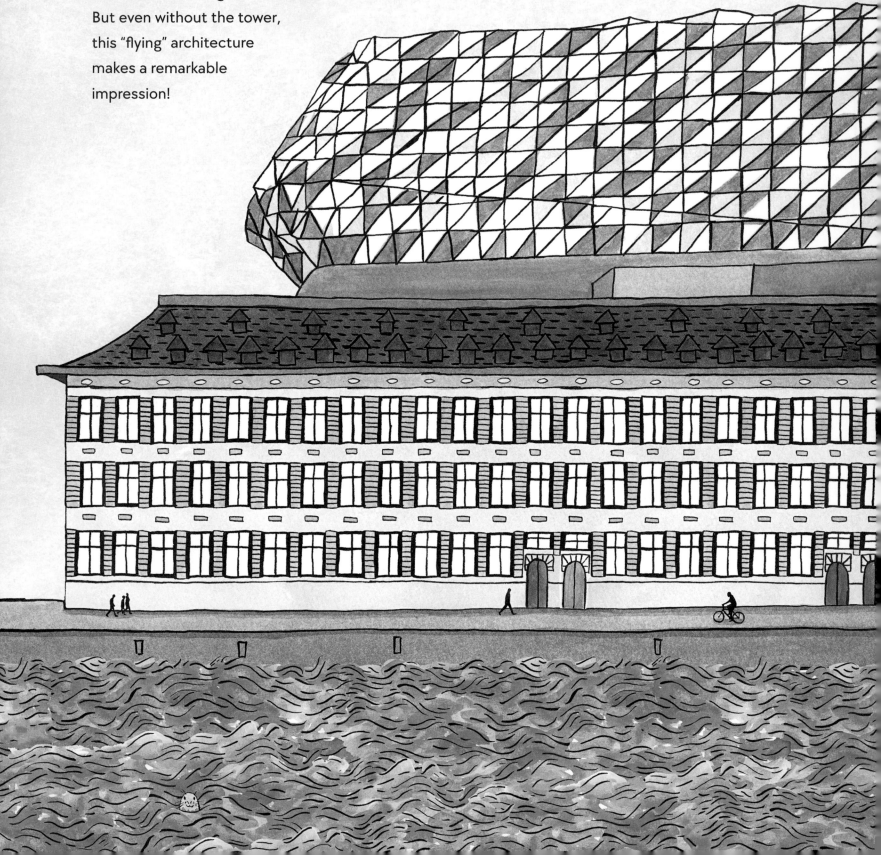

Port House Antwerp

A harbor building like a flying whale

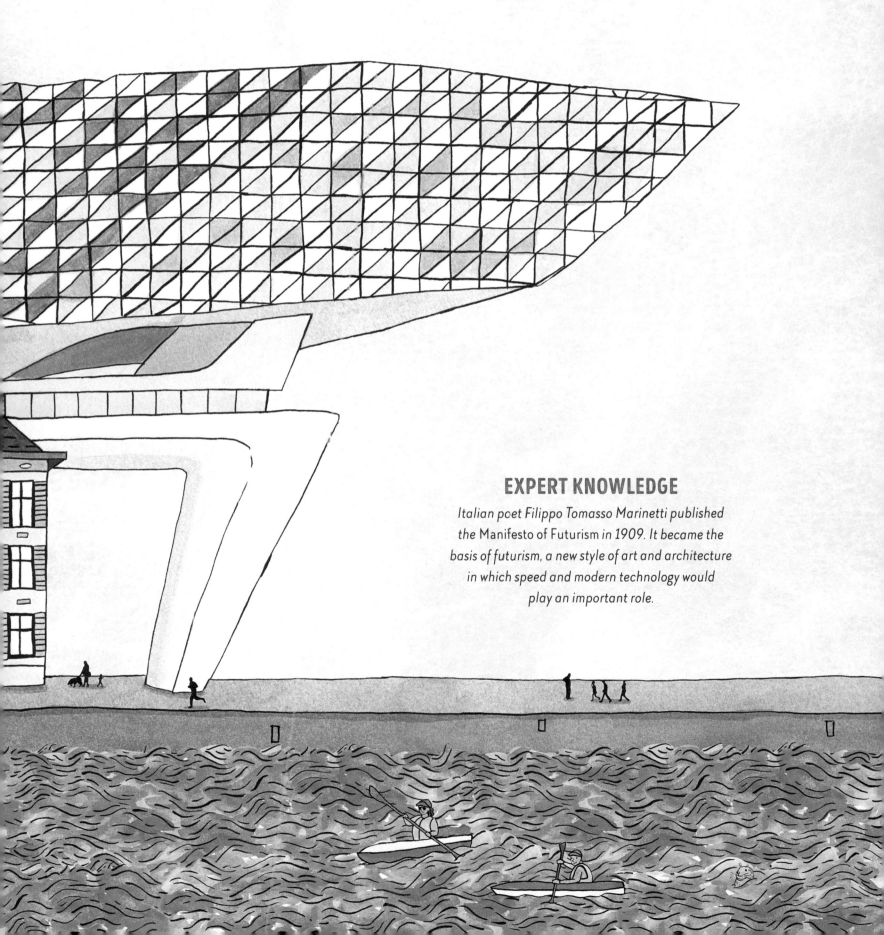

EXPERT KNOWLEDGE

Italian poet Filippo Tomasso Marinetti published the Manifesto of Futurism in 1909. It became the basis of futurism, a new style of art and architecture in which speed and modern technology would play an important role.

The original name of this gallery—"Husain-Doshi ni Gufa"—sums up its history. Artist Maqbool Fida Husain and architect Balkrishna Vihaldas Doshi, both from India, had discussed the advantages of underground spaces in view of their country's hot climate. Thirty years after their conversation, they created a great work of art now called the Amdavad ni Gufa. This remarkable art gallery lies mostly underground, like a cave. *Gufa* is an Indian word meaning "grotto". The gallery's white, tile-clad domes can only be seen partially from outside. Mosaic images of black snakes crawl along the tops of the domes, a creation of M.F. Husain. The gallery's entrance discreetly leads into a wonderful world full of bright colors, tree-like buttresses, and sculptures by Husain.

Amdavad ni Gufa

A gallery like a stalactite cave

Fagus Factory

A factory like a modern villa

When UNESCO designates a structure to be a world heritage site, it must be very, very special. These buildings include the ancient Egyptian pyramids of Giza and the Great Wall of China. Only cultural sites with a value for the whole world become heritage sites, and one of these places is the Fagus Factory!

German entrepreneur Carl Benscheidt engaged a young architect named Walter Gropius to design a factory for making shoe lasts (shoe-shaped wooden tools used to make and repair shoes). The building was meant to provide ideal conditions for the workers and be bright and friendly.

Gropius, who later went on to co-establish the famous Bauhaus school of design, had already developed a type of 'curtain wall' made of steel columns and glass. With this technology, he could build enormous windows that reached the corners of the building without thick wall supports. By using these innovations, the Fagus Factory helped kick-start a new era in architecture—modernism!

ADDITIONAL INFO

"Fagus" comes from the Latin term for beech wood, the material used to make traditional shoes lasts!

AND ANOTHER TIP

You can see many photos of this building at fagus-werk.com.

It's no wonder that Danish architect Jørn Utzon immediately thought of white sails when he entered a competition to design the opera house for Sydney, Australia. After all, the planned site was on a headland in the city's harbor, and Utzon's father was a yacht builder. The young architect only submitted sketchy initial designs, but these drawings won him the commission over more than 230 other entries. Once Utzon's plans were accepted, it was up to Ove Nyquist Arup, a British engineer, to make sure the futuristic structure could be built securely and safely. When visiting the opera house today, people can enjoy five theater halls, one movie theater, four restaurants, as well as bars, shops and the required ancillary rooms. All of these facilities lie under 14 shell-shaped roofs, each of which is covered in 1.1 million ceramic tiles. Four hundred miles of power cables are needed to supply this small city of culture! Jørn Utzon, however, was not allowed to complete his opera house. Due to ever-increasing construction costs, he got involved in a dispute with the Australian government and left the country a few years before completion. His name was not even mentioned at the opening ceremony. But Utzon accepted an apology in 1999 and took care of the building's renovation work. Today, there is a hall named after him, and his Sydney Opera House has even made it onto the final list for the modern wonders of the world!

Sydney Opera House

An opera house hoists its sails

EXPERT KNOWLEDGE

A structural engineer calculates the forces that act on buildings and knows how strong a material must be to make a building safe!

TIP

*Grab an old box made of not-too-thick
cardboard, a pair of scissors, and some glue,
and let your imagination run free.
What does your emergency shelter look like?*

Shelter of Cardboard
A shelter like a moving box

There are events, such as wars or natural disasters,
that force people to move from their homes, whether
they want to or not. They may not even get a chance to pack
their bags or look for a new place to stay. Such misfortunes often result
in hastily constructed refugee camps, where the most necessary things like
washing facilities, bathrooms, secure pathways, and doors are unavailable.
Maybe you've seen these camps on television or online.

Every now and again, halls are re-purposed so that people can at least stay
dry. One architect, Shigeru Ban from Japan, has developed a new, more
humane idea for building refugee camps. He invented small huts made
from cardboard rolls to provide people with as dignified a refuge as possible,
despite their terrible circumstances. These pleasant-looking huts are
inexpensive, easy to assemble and dismantle, and can be set up in a sports
hall or even placed on a foundation of beer crates. Sometimes, even the
humblest buildings can make great art!

Tree House

A residential tower block like an enchanted garden

More than 2,500 years ago, legendary Babylonian queen Semiramis decided she would live in both a palace and the middle of nature at the same time. That's why she had the Hanging Gardens erected, a huge building with magnificently planted terraces. According to another theory, the hanging gardens were not even requested by Semiramis, but that does not matter. For their times, these roof gardens were such an amazing engineering feat that they counted among the seven wonders of the ancient world.

Today, modern materials and computer technology have enabled architects to design ever more elaborate structures, but the desire to have more nature in cities has not changed. As early as the 1960s, Singapore's urban planners set out to create the greenest city in the world, and they're well on their way to achieving that dream today! An outstanding part of this project is the Tree House, which should really be called the 'Towering Tree', as it goes up 24 storeys! As you can see, the building's garden has been planted right on the façade. This feature not only looks pretty, but it also improves air quality, stores rainwater, saves energy, reduces air conditioning costs and creates a wonderful living space for the inhabitants of the apartments, as well as for local animal and plant life.

TIP

How would you like to build a skyscraper for insects?
First, collect some hollow wood, sticks, pinecones,
and everything else that little creatures can crawl into.
Next, glue your findings together and bind them
with some wire.

Micro Yuan'er

A children's library that could not be prettier

As is the case with all major cities, land in the center of Beijing, China, is at a premium. That's why the city's centuries-old *hutongs* (a type of narrow street with small courtyard houses) are being torn down and replaced by modern, tall buildings. Many older hutong residents can no longer afford to live there, so they've been forced to move to the outskirts of Beijing. Chinese architect Zhang Ke is campaigning against this so-called urban renewal.

When Zhang gets a commission, he takes a good look at the place where the building is meant to be and finds out what the people there need. One such project involved a 350-year-old tea house in an old Beijing hutong. Zhang felt this building could offer a place of togetherness, especially for children. That's why he came up with a tiny cultural center. In the 20-square-foot showroom of an old kitchen, which occupies the central area of a courtyard, you can now climb up an outside staircase and sit among the leaves of a tree. A small library made of plywood is housed under the historical roof. Using these design ideas, Zhang Ke was able to retain the old and combine it with the new. Is there any nicer form of togetherness?

Fagus Factory

Location: Alfeld, Germany
Architect: Walter Gropius
Construction: 1911
Type: Shoe last factory
Material: Reinforced concrete,
brick construction,
curtain wall
See page 46

Einstein Tower

Location: Potsdam, Germany
Architects: Erich Mendelsohn;
Outside facilities, Richard Neutra
Construction: 1924
Type: Solar observatory
Material: Steel, reinforced concrete,
brick masonry
Style: Expressionism
See page 34

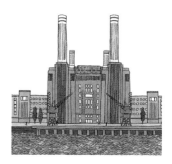

Battersea Power Station

Location: London, United Kingdom
Architect: Giles Gilbert Scott
Opened: Section A (first two
chimneys only), 1933; Section B, 1948
Type: Conversion of a power station
into a mixed use building
Material: Steel skeletal
structure with brick infill
Style: Art Deco
See page 26

—1911——————————1924———————————1933/1948—

Walter Gropius ...

was born in Germany's capital city, Berlin, in 1883 and died in Boston, USA in 1969. Together with Le Corbusier and Frank Lloyd Wright, he was one of the pioneers of modern architecture. He also founded the Bauhaus, a world-famous art and design studio in Weimar, Germany, in 1919. These achievements are all the more remarkable because Gropius was terrible at drawing—so bad, in fact, that he quit his university architecture studies!
As head of the Bauhaus, Walter had staff members help him convert his ideas—everything from buildings to door handles—into real-life objects. "You see," he said "Anyone can become an architect. The main thing is you have good ideas!"

Erich Mendelsohn ...

was born in Allenstein, Germany (now Olsztyn, Poland) in 1887. After initially training as a commercial clerk, Erich studied architecture. Soon, he was planning many unusual buildings, such as a hat factory in Luckenwalde, which looked like a hat when viewed from one side. Erich became much in demand as an architect and was awash with commissions. In 1933, however, the National Socialists (the Nazis) took power in Germany, and Mendelsohn, who was Jewish, could no longer work in a country that discriminated against Jews. He fled to Palestine that year and eventually made his way to the United States. In America, his buildings were partly influenced by Frank Lloyd Wright, the architect of Fallingwater. It's never wrong to learn something from the talented people in your field and then put your own spin on it!

Richard Neutra ...

was born in Vienna, Austria in 1882. After studying architecture and architectural landscape design, he immigrated to the United States. Like many of his colleagues, Neutra became a big fan of Frank Lloyd Wright. He even named his son after this great master of architecture! Many of Neutra's designs followed the principles of Wright's buildings, as well as that of the European international style, a style popularized by architects like Walter Gropius. One good example of his work is the Desert House in Palm Springs, California. Although Neutra was more highly valued in America than in Europe, he designed several houses in France, Germany, and Switzerland at the end of his life. He died of a heart attack in Wuppertal, Germany, in 1980 while viewing one of these houses.

Giles Gilbert Scott ...

was born in London in 1880 and died there in 1960. His mother was of the view that, as a member of a family with many successful architects, Giles should also become one himself. Her son agreed. At just 22 years of age, he won a design competition for the new Liverpool Cathedral. This project became a huge undertaking that would occupy much of his life. Scott abandoned his original designs and produced new ones at different points over the next several decades. He came to believe that the new cathedral, which was originally based on a centuries-old Gothic style, should also appear modern. Evolving your own style over time can make you a better architect!

Gosplan Garage

Location: Moscow, Russia
Architect: Konstantin Melnikov
Construction: approx. 1935
Type: Garage with workshops,
office space, and refectory
Material: Reinforced concrete
Style: Futurism (Constructivism)
Special feature: One of the few
surviving buildings of the
Soviet avant-garde
See page 20

Fallingwater
(Kaufmann-House)

Location: Mill Run,
Pennsylvania, USA
Architect: Frank Lloyd Wright
Construction period:
1935–1939
Type: Weekend house
Material: Reinforced concrete
with glass and natural stone
See page 22

Unité d'Habitation

Location: Marseille, France
and Berlin, Germany
(also originally in Rizé, Briey
and Firminy, France)
Architect: Charles-Édouard Jeanneret-Gris,
also known as Le Corbusier
Construction period: 1947–1965
Type: Residential apartments
Material: Reinforced concrete
Style: Brutalism
Special features: The Unité's proportions,
known as the *modulor*, are based
on human measurements.
See page 6

━1935━━━━━━━━━━━1935–1939━━━━━━━━━━1947–1965━

Konstantin Melnikov ...

was born in Moscow, Russia, in 1890 and died there in 1974. He came from a poor family, but his father noticed his talent for design and gave him paper for drawing. One day, Konstantin's drawings were shown to a local engineer. He was so impressed that he gave Melnikov a job at his firm and helped him to go to school and study architecture. Konstantin was soon designing buildings that looked like sculptures, some of which were constructed shortly after Russia became a new country called the Soviet Union. By the 1930's, however, Soviet leaders wanted buildings that were more conservative, and they would reject Melnikov's architecture as sheer fantasies. Today, only a few of his buildings remain standing. One of these is his own house, the Melnikov House in Moscow.

Frank Lloyd Wright ...

was born in the town of Richland Center, Wisconsin, USA in 1867, and he died in Phoenix, Arizona in 1959. Even though Wright never finished his architecture studies, he became a teacher and inspiration for countless architects who went on to become famous themselves. Wright established a farm with work-rooms in the middle of the Wisconsin prairie and invited students from all over the world to attend his workshops. He called this place Taliesin, which sounds like a name from a fantasy novel! In fact, it's a Welsh term meaning "shining brow." The Taliesin farm was built into the "brow" (or top) of a hill.

Charles-Édouard Jeanneret-Gris, known as Le Corbusier...

was born in La Chaux-de-Fonds, Switzerland in 1887 and died in Roquebrune-Cap-Martin, France in 1965. Architects around the world value him as one of the most important masters of modern architecture. Corbusier's designs were completely different from the fancy, elaborately decorated buildings of his youth. Just compare his Villa Savoye with other single-family homes from the late 1800s or early 1900s (get a grown-up to help you find photos on the internet). By using columns and roof gardens, he made it possible to create open floor plans and unusually-shaped facades. Even a hundred years later, Corbusier's ideas can be used by architects who want to build sustainably.

TWA Flight Center New York

Location: JFK Airport, New York, USA
Architect: Eero Saarinen
Opened: 1962
Type: Airport terminal
Material: Reinforced concrete, glass
See page 8

Munich Olympic Stadium

Location: Munich, Germany
Architects: Günter Behnisch,
Frei Otto, and many of
Behnisch's staff members
Opened: 1972
Type: Stadium
Material: Steel, plexiglass
Style: Organic architecture
Special feature: A so-called
"earth stadium," embedded
in the ground
See page 14

Sydney Opera House

Location: Sydney, Australia
Architect: Jørn Utzon
Opened: 1973
Type: Opera house
Material: Reinforced concrete,
prefabricated concrete,
granite slabs
Style: Organic architecture
See page 48

1962 ———————— **1972** ———————— **1973**

Eero Saarinen ...

was born in Kirkkonummi, Finland in 1910 and died in Ann Arbor, Michigan, USA in 1961. Eero's family immigrated to America when he was only thirteen years old, and he received his early artistic training in sculpture. He then studied architecture and joined the architectural firm of his father, Eliel. You can see from Eero's buildings that he always had sculptural shapes in mind. Even his smaller furniture designs, such as the famous Tulip Chair, look like sculptures. It's no surprise, therefore, that he greatly admired Jørn Utzon's sculptural design for the Sydney Opera House. Eero was a juror for that building's design competition, and he helped convince the jury to award Utzon the commission.

Günter Behnisch ...

was born in Lockwitz, near Dresden, Germany in 1922 and died in Stuttgart, Germany in 2010. He disliked buildings that were designed to show off the wealth or power of their clients. Instead, Behnisch created feather-light structures, such as the Plenary Hall in Bonn and the Hysolar Institute Building in Stuttgart. Because of his liberal attitude toward architecture, Behnisch is often referred to as the "Master Builder of Democracy."

Frei Otto ...

was born in Siegmar, near Chemnitz, Germany in 1925 and died in Leonberg, Germany in 2015. His mother chose the wonderful first name of Frei for him because it represents her motto in life (*frei* means "free" in German). And to be as free as a bird, Frei decided to take up gliding, a hobby that would help him discover the versatile lightness of skin-like surfaces. He would use such surfaces in many of his buildings, including the bird aviary at Hellabrunn Zoo in Munich. Otto's firm also helped pioneer ecologically minded building practices—practices that wasted as little space, materials, and energy as possible.

Jørn Utzon ...

was born in Copenhagen, Denmark in 1918 and died there in 2008. As a young student, he was never very good at math, and he was rejected from the Royal Danish Naval Academy. Jørn had wanted to become a naval officer. Fortunately, he changed his mind and went on to study architecture. His wonderful building designs often appear as light as sailing ships!

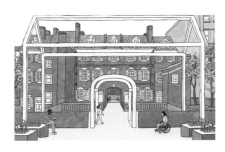

Franklin Court

Location: Philadelphia, Pennsylvania, USA
Architects: Denise Scott Brown
and Robert Venturi
Opened: 1976
Type: Open memorial site
Material: Painted steel
Style: Post-modernism
See page 30

SESC Pompéia

Location: São Paulo, Brazil
Architect: Lina Bo Bardi
Opened: 1986
Type: Leisure center
Material: Exposed concrete
Special feature: Conversion of an
existing structure for a new purpose
See page 12

Amdavad ni Gufa

Location: Ahmedabad, India
Architect: Balkrishna Doshi
Construction period: 1992–1995
Type: Art gallery
Material: Iron cement, mosaic tiles
Style: Organic architecture
See page 44

—1976— —1986— —1992—

Denise Scott Brown ...

was born in Nkana, Northern Rhodesia, in 1931. She studied architecture in South Africa and London. Together with her second husband, Robert Venturi, she wrote important books on architectural theory, which influenced many of her colleagues. She said quite modestly that architects should not play god. Robert Venturi won the famous Pritzker Prize for their joint work, but a request that the prize be awarded to Scott Brown as well was declined. This decision was not fair! Nonetheless, Denise took the rejection calmly.

Robert Venturi ...

was born in Philadelphia, Pennsylvania, USA in 1925 and died there in 2018. He and his wife, Denise Scott Brown, designed many famous buildings, including a house for his mother, Vanna. This home has been described as one of the "biggest small buildings" of the late 1900s. Venturi and Scott Brown also wrote books on architecture, which became even more influential than their buildings. Robert was always looking at the buildings around him, and he described them as either "ducks" or "decorated sheds". A duck building has a special form or shape that indicates its purpose, while a decorated shed is an ordinary building that needs signs or decoration on the outside to tell people what goes on inside. Ideas such as these became part of an architectural movement called post-modernism.

Lina Bo Bardi ...

was born in Rome, Italy in 1914, where she studied architecture, even though it was considered a "male profession" at that time. She often cared little about what others expected of her. That's why she immigrated with her husband to São Paulo, Brazil, where she was able to work more freely until her death in 1992. Bo Bardi's independent spirit can be seen in her buildings, such as the Museu de Arte and her own house, the Casa de Vidro (Glass House). It was important for her to merge architecture and nature, and she designed green facades and hanging gardens long before they were fashionable among her colleagues!

Balkrishna Vithaldas Doshi ...

was born in Pune, India in 1927. Though his firm and architectural school are in India, Doshi has been inspired by famous architects from all over the world, such as Le Corbusier. He maintains that that you have to think big, but also "be rooted so that you can bloom." Doshi's own "blooms" were seen in major projects such as the Aranya Low Cost Housing development, a multi-thousand-unit residential complex in which residents could encounter each other on shared stairwells.

Jean-Marie Tjibaou Cultural Center

Location: Nouméa, New Caledonia in the South Pacific
Architect: Renzo Piano
Construction period: 1993–1998
Type: Cultural center
Material: Iroko wood, stainless steel, concrete
Style: Organic architecture
Special feature: Considered the forerunner of green architecture
See page 10

Shelter of Cardboard

Location: Wherever it is needed
Architect: Shigeru Ban
Construction: Whenever it is needed
Type: Shelter
Material: Cardboard rolls, canvass, beverage crates
See page 50

Dirty House

Location: Shoreditch district, London, United Kingdom
Architect: Sir David Adjaye
Construction period: 2001–2002
Type: Conversion of a warehouse into a residential and studio building
Material: Brick with anti-graffiti bitumen paint, steel, glass
See page 28

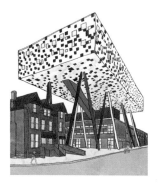

Sharp Center for Design

Location: Toronto, Canada
Architect: Will Alsop
Opened: 2004
Type: University building
Material: Steel columns, aluminum skin
See page 32

—1993–1998— —1995— —2001–2002— —2004—

Renzo Piano ...

was born into a family of timber merchants in Genoa, Italy in 1937, so it was fitting that he wanted to study architecture. He named his firm Renzo Piano Building Workshop because, for him, architecture always means teamwork and not the creation of a single person. Renzo and his colleagues have designed buildings throughout Europe and North America, and no one design is like the other!

Shigeru Ban ...

was born in Tokyo in 1957 and still lives and works there today. The Transitional Cathedral in Christchurch, New Zealand and the Pompidou Center in Metz, France show his creative use of building materials. For example, the cathedral's walls are made, in part, from giant cardboard tubes. To support people in need, Ban set up a network of voluntary architects. With their expert knowledge, they help provide shelter for people who have lost their homes in wars or natural catastrophes.

David Adjaye ...

was born in Daressalam, Tanzania in 1966 and lives and works in London. As a child, he travelled a lot with his parents and managed to gather many influences for his professional career. Architecture, in his opinion, should be a kind of "Robin Hood," in that it provides usefulness for those with little money. After building many successful works, such as the large Museum of Contemporary Art in Denver and the small Elektra House in London, he was knighted by Britain's Queen Elizabeth II as Sir David Adjaye. The queen does not give that honor to everyone!

Will(iam) Alsop ...

was born in London, England in 1947 and died there in 2018. He was also a painter, which helps explain his unusually shaped and colorful buildings, such as Peckham Library in London or the Colorium, a multi-colored skyscraper in Düsseldorf, Germany. Alsop believed that artists should not always know the result of their works beforehand, which is why he preferred to capture the initial ideas for his spirited architectural designs in pictures before he set about their execution!

New Museum of Contemporary Art

Location: New York, USA
Architects: Kazuyo Sejima and
Ryūe Nishizawa (SAANA)
Opened: 2007
Type: Art museum
Materia : Steel skeletal frame,
stretched aluminum facade
Style: Minimalism
See page 16

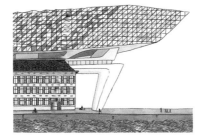

Port House Antwerp

Location: Antwerp, Belgium
Architect: Zaha Hadid
Construction: 2010
Type: Administration building
Material: Aluminum
Style: Neo-Futurism
See page 42

Steilneset Memorial

Location: Vardø, Norway
Architect: Peter Zumthor
Artist: Louise Bourgeois
Opened: 2011
Type: Memorial site with museum
Material: Wood and canvass,
steel and glass
Special feature: This architecture
of contrasts does not explain;
it just touches on the truth!
See page 18

— 2007 — 2010 — 2011 —

Kazuyo Sejima ...

was born in 1956 in Hitachi, Japan. She studied architecture in Tokyo at a private university for women, which was founded over one hundred years ago and is a place where many famous Japanese artists have trained. Kazuyo's simple yet elegant structures are in great demand all over the world. They include the Zollverein Cole Mine Industrial Complex in Essen, Germany and the Hokusai Museum Sumida in Tokyo, which she is planning with her partner, Ryūe Nishizawa. Both she and Ryūe won the prestigious Pritzker Architecture Prize. She was also the first woman to direct the Venice Biennale of Architecture, a world-famous exhibition for architects.

Ryūe Nishizawa ...

was born in Kanagawa Prefecture, Japan in 1966. Together with his former boss Kazuyo Sejima, he founded the SAANA architectural firm in Tokyo. The two architects designed many successful buildings, and they eventually won the coveted Pritzker Architecture Prize together, a rare accomplishment. Any team that can create architecture that is "both unique and inspirational," as the Pritzker jury declared, deserves an award!

Zaha Hadid ...

was born in Baghdad, Iraq in 1950 and died at just 66 years of age in Miami, Florida, USA in 2016. In 2004, she became the first female winner of the Pritzker Prize, the world's most prestigious architecture award. Hadid's parents supported their daughter's talents from an early age. Even as an 11-year-old, Zaha was allowed to design her own furnishings for her room. She did them so well, in fact, that her family's carpenter went on to make the furniture for other children. However, Zaha's designs for houses were so crazy that clients did not dare realize them. One client even rejected a design that won a competition three times in a row! What can we learn from Zaha's story? Never give up!

Peter Zumthor ...

was born in Basel, Switzerland in 1943. Before studying architecture, he completed an apprenticeship in carpentry at his father's workshop. Zumthor's first architectural job was as a monument conservator, a person who helps care for and preserve very old buildings. He then began work on his own projects, such as the Thermal Baths in Vals, Switzerland, and the Kunsthaus Museum in Bregenz, Austria, which became renowned globally and won him the coveted Pritzker Prize. You can see how thoroughly the architect worked on the details of these projects. Even the roof shingles are carefully designed!

Louise Bourgeois ...

was born in 1911 in Paris, France and died a world-renowned artist in New York in 2010. Her mother, with whom she had a better relationship than with her father, worked as a weaver. In her mother's honor, Louise created huge bronze spiders, which she affectionately called "Maman". In her eyes, art is a "guarantee for sanity." Let's follow her advice and get out our paint brushes!

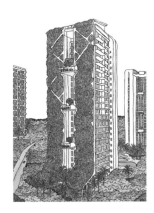

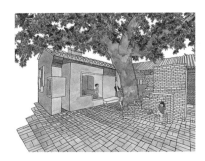

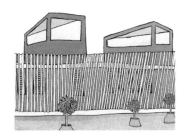

Tree House

Location: Singapore
Architect: ADDP architects LLP
Construction: 2014
Type: High-rise building with
condominiums
Material: Reinforced concrete,
vine plants
Style: Green architecture
See page 52

Micro Yuan'er Children's Library and Art Centre

Location: Beijing, China
Architect: Ke Zhang
Construction: 2014
Type: Children's library
Material: Concrete, plywood,
glass, blue-gray bricks
Style: Minimalism
See page 54

Lycée Schorge

Location: Koudougou,
Burkina Faso
Architect: Diébédo Francis Kéré
Opened: 2016
Type: School
Material: Laterite stone,
sheet metal, wood
See page 40

—— 2014 —————— 2014 —————— 2016 ——

ADDP architects LLP

is an architectural practice founded in Singapore in 1986 and run by Chin Hang Pin and Lim Meng Hwa. It was one of the first design firms to receive an ISO14001 certificate. This certificate sounds pretty technical, but it shows that the architects have made buildings that help protect the environment!

Ke Zhang ...

was born in China in 1970. He founded a well-known architecture and design studio called ZAO/standardarchitecture. Zhang believes that architects should never forget who will live in their buildings when they design them, regardless of what their clients want. You can see that principle in his buildings, which never appear flashy and always blend into their environment and reflect the history of their location!

Diébédo Francis Kéré ...

was born in 1965 in Gando, a small village in Burkina Faso. After completing an apprenticeship in carpentry and learning the traditional building techniques of his homeland, he studied architecture in Germany, where he now runs his architectural firm. He also teaches at several European universities. As an architect, Kéré prefers to design schools, health centers, and other buildings in his native Africa—structures that can benefit local people and be constructed with local and ecologically sound materials.

CopenHill
(Amager Bakke)

Location: Copenhagen, Denmark
Architect: Bjarke Ingels
(BIG – Bjarke Ingels Group) and
SLA Landscape Architects
Opened: 2017
Type: Refuse incineration plant,
power station, leisure park
Material: Steel, cement, aluminum
Special feature: Hybrid building
with a variety of functions
See page 24

Elbe Philharmonic
Hall

Location: Hamburg, Germany
Architects: Jacques Herzog and
Pierre de Meuron
Opened: 2017
Type: Concert hall
Material: Steel, reinforced concrete,
brick masonry
See page 36

Regional Market

Location: Dandaji, Niger
Architect: Mariam Kamara
Opened: 2018
Type: Market enclosure
Material: CEB bricks,
recycled metal
See page 38

— 2017 — — 2017 — — 2018 —

Bjarke Ingels ...

was born in the Danish capital city of
Copenhagen in 1974. Becoming an
architect was not his first idea of a dream
job. Ingels originally wanted to be a comic
book illustrator, creating fantasy worlds
with just pen and paper. Today, he runs
the BIG (Bjarke-Ingels-Group) architecture
firm, and he can see his designs take
shape in the real world. Whether it is the
award-winning VIA 57 West in New York
City or the Maritime Museum of Helsingør,
Denmark, his structures are rarely small
or modest, but they're all absolute
eye-catchers. All the same, sustainability
is an important theme with his buildings.
Bjarke has also made a book about
architecture designed like a comic book!

Jaques Herzog and
Pierre de Meuron ...

were both born in Basel, Switzerland in
1950. Friends from elementary school, the
two men studied architecture together
before setting up their own design
studio—a studio that has become one of
the largest and more famous in the world.
Today, around 400 staff members take
care of the designs for major projects such
as the Allianz Arena, a soccer stadium
in Munich, Germany, or the extension of
the Tate Modern art museum in London.
Maybe you would like to become famous
with one of your own friends?

Mariam Kamara ...

was born in St. Etienne, France in 1979,
but her family returned shortly after her
birth to their homeland of Niger. Although
she lives in Boston, she founded her
studio in Niamey, Niger's capital city.
Kamara is bold enough to tell her clients
things that she believes are good for
them, for architecture, and for the
environment. Mariam's friend and former
teacher, Sir David Adjaye, says about her:
"She is a pioneer. She lives as a Muslim
woman in a culture that does not reckon
on such an instigator." Kamara plans
sustainable, highly modern structures
like the Niamey Cultural Center, which
adapt many traditional Nigerien building
methods. Her work also encourages other
young women from Africa to follow in her
footsteps.

Annette Roeder ...

is an architect and illustrator and
author of numerous children's
books as well as novels for adults.
She lives with her family on the
outskirts of Munich, Germany.

Pamela Baron ...

is a freelance illustrator and artist who
has a special love of architecture.
She holds a BFA in illustration from the
Rhode Island School of Design and
currently lives in a breezy town outside
of San Francisco with her husband
and twenty-one miniature fruit trees.
This is her second children's book.

© 2022, Prestel Verlag, Munich · London · New York
A member of Penguin Random House
Verlagsgruppe GmbH
Neumarkter Strasse 28 · 81673 Munich
Text: Annette Roeder
Illustrations: Pamela Baron

© for the works held by the artists or their legal
heirs except for: © ADCK – centre culturel Tjibaou/
RPBW: Jean-Marie Tjibaou Cultural Center;
Illustrations of Fallingwater used with permission of
the Western Pennsylvania Conservancy.
We thank all institutions and companies for their
kind permission.

Library of Congress Control Number: 2022935168
A CIP catalogue record for this book is available
from the British Library.

Translated from the German by Paul Kelly

Editorial direction: Doris Kutschbach
Copyediting: Brad Finger
Design and layout: Meike Sellier
Production management: Susanne Hermann
Separations: Reproline Mediateam, Munich
Printing and binding: TBB, a.s., Slovakia

Prestel Publishing compensates the CO_2
emissions produced from the making of this
book by supporting a reforestation project
in Brazil. Find further information on the project
here: www.ClimatePartner.com/14044-1912-1001

Penguin Random House Verlagsgruppe
FSC® N001967

ISBN 978-3-7913-7514-4
www.prestel.com